M000189445

Your Grief
and
God's Promises

Your Grief
and
God's Promises

Words of Comfort and Hope
for the Grieving Christian

By Criswell Freeman

DELANEY STREET PRESS; Nashville, TN: (800) 256-8584

ISBN 1-58334-084-X

The ideas expressed in this book are not, in all cases, exact quotations, as some have been edited for clarity and brevity. In all cases, the author has attempted to maintain the speaker's original intent. In some cases, material for this book was obtained from secondary sources, primarily print media. While every effort was made to ensure the accuracy of these sources, the accuracy cannot be guaranteed. For additions, deletions, corrections or clarifications in future editions of this text, please write DELANEY STREET PRESS.

All scripture verses, unless otherwise indicated, are taken from the KING JAMES VERSION of the Holy Bible.

Scripture quotations taken from the HOLY BIBLE, NEW INTERNATIONAL VERSION©, NIV©, Copyright 1973, 1978, 1984, by International Bible Society. Used by permission of Zondervan Publishing House. All rights reserved.

Scripture taken from the NEW AMERICAN STANDARD BIBLE ®, Copyright ©1960, 1962, 1963, 1968, 1971, 1973, 1975, 1977, 1995 by the Lockman Foundation. Used by permission.

Printed in the United States of America
Cover Design by Bart Dawson
Typesetting & Page Layout by Sue Gerdes

2 3 4 5 6 7 8 9 10 • 00 01 02 03 04 05 06

ACKNOWLEDGMENTS

The author gratefully acknowledges the helpful support of Angela Beasley Freeman, Dick and Mary Freeman, Mary Susan Freeman, Jim Gallery, and the entire team of professionals at DELANEY STREET PRESS and WALNUT GROVE PRESS.

For Those Who Mourn

Table of Contents

Have courage for all
the great sorrows of life
and patience for the
small ones. And when
you have finished your
daily task, go to sleep.
God is awake.

Victor Hugo

Introduction

In time, grief visits us all. We experience some deeply significant loss: perhaps the death of a loved one; perhaps the loss of health; perhaps divorce, job loss, or a broken personal relationship. Whatever the nature of the loss, its pain is so profound that we honestly wonder if recovery is possible.

The Christian faith, as communicated through the words of the Holy Bible, is a healing faith. It offers comfort in times of trouble, courage for our fears, hope instead of hopelessness. For Christians, the grave is not a final resting place. Through the healing words of God's promises, Christians understand that the Lord continues to manifest His plan in good times and bad.

If you are experiencing the intense pain of a recent loss, or if you are still mourning a loss from long ago, this book is intended to help. These pages contain relevant Bible verses along with the healing words of knowledgeable men and women, many of whom are experts in grief counseling. This collection of verses and quotations is intended to provide you with an understanding of the grieving process and with renewed hope for the future.

Grief is not meant to be avoided or feared, it is meant to be worked through. If this book, in some small way, assists you as you move through and beyond your pain, it will have served its purpose. May God bless you and keep you, and may He place his healing hand upon your heart today and forever.

Part I
Your Grief

1

Understanding Your Grief

Grief is a uniquely personal experience. But grief is also a universal experience, a journey that has been clearly mapped by those who have documented the common elements of human suffering.

Grief usually begins with shock and then gives way to intense pain. Over time, as the mourner regains his or her emotional balance, the pain begins to fade. Gradually, a new life is raised from the ashes of the old. Christians face grief armed with God's promises. Through the Holy Bible, He promises to comfort and heal those who call upon Him.

As you experience the searing pain of any significant loss, knowledge is power. The more you understand the grieving process, the better you can cope with its many twists and turns. But whatever the nature of your loss, always remember this overriding truth: God is with you, God is good, and you are protected.

The stage of shock and numbness is so common that it is predictable. It may be Nature's cloak of protection.

Genevieve Davis Ginsburg

When the full impact of our loss hit home, it seemed that everything moved in slow motion.

Zig Ziglar

O Lord God of my salvation, I have cried day and night before thee...for my soul is full of trouble.
Psalm: 88:1-3

Do not be afraid of the shock that
often comes with the early stages of grief.
Granger Westberg

The shock phase, for all its confusion,
helps us adapt by forming an insulation
against the chaotic outside world.
Catherine M. Sanders

Be not afraid, only believe.
Mark 5:36

Grief is the aftermath of any deeply
significant loss.
Wayne Oates

Grief is the pain of mind, produced
by loss, misfortune, injury, or evils
of any kind.
Noah Webster

*We must through much tribulation enter into the
kingdom of heaven.*
Acts 14:22

Grief is a journey, a pilgrimage —
   something we pass through.

James W. Moore

Grief is a natural part
      of human experience.

Granger Westberg

*Trouble and anguish have taken hold on me:
   yet thy commandments are my delight.
   Psalm 119:143*

Grief is always more than sorrow.
It is a rawness you feel at the center
of your being.
Harriet Sarnoff Schiff

Grief affects us spiritually, physically,
socially, and in every other facet of life.
Zig Ziglar

Fear thou not; for I am with thee: be not dismayed
for I am thy God: I will strengthen thee.
Isaiah 41:10

God whispers to us in our pleasures,
speaks in our conscience, but shouts
in our pain.

C. S. Lewis

It is such a secret place,
the land of tears.

Antoine de Saint-Exupéry

I am not alone, because the Father is with me.
John 16:32

Earth has no sorrow that heaven cannot heal.

Thomas More

God shall wipe away all the tears from their eyes.
Revelations: 7:17

2

Expressing Your Emotions

God gave you emotions for a reason. When you express those emotions sincerely, you begin the process of healing. But if you suppress your emotions or ignore them altogether, you may needlessly prolong your own suffering.

If you have experienced a significant loss, grieve it. Express your feelings; allow tears to flow; share your sadness with others; acknowledge your pain. By honestly expressing your grief, you are taking an active role in God's plan for your recovery.

Giving yourself permission to grieve is a great gift.

Bob Deits

O Lord my God, I cried unto thee,
and thou hast healed me.
Psalm 30:2

Tears are the natural form of release
for the still-suppressed feelings of love and
gratitude, and also for the reservoir of pain
and sorrow we have in our hearts.

Zig Ziglar

To weep is to make less the depth of grief.
William Shakespeare

*Weeping may endure for a night, but joy cometh
in the morning.
Psalm 30:5*

Most mourners report that from time to time they have wondered whether it is worth it to adapt or readjust to their loss.

Glen W. Davidson

Sorrow is what we feel. It is that inner sadness we carry with us as we go about our daily lives.

Harriet Sarnoff Schiff

O my God, my soul is cast down within me: therefore I will remember thee....
Psalm 42:6

Weeping is only a stage — it won't last forever so you needn't be afraid to cry.

Alla Renée Bozarth

There is certain joy in weeping
for by tears, grief is relieved.

Ovid

*Ye shall be sorrowful, but your sorrow
shall be turned into joy.*
John 16:20

A teardrop on earth
summons the King
of heaven.

Charles Swindoll

*Blessed are they that mourn:
for they shall be comforted.
Matthew 5:4*

Tears are as natural as laughter
    and just as healing.
                Kathlyn S. Baldwin

Tears from the depths of some divine
    despair rise in the heart
    and gather to the eyes.
                Alfred, Lord Tennyson

A time to weep and a time to laugh;
A time to mourn and a time to dance.
        Ecclesiastes 3: 4 NASB

God has a bottle and a book for his people's tears. What was sown as a tear will come up as a pearl.

Matthew Henry

Tears clean the windows of the soul.

Pearl Barker

Cast your burden upon the Lord
and He will sustain you.
Psalm 55:22 NASB

We should be thankful for our tears; they prepare us for a clearer vision of God.

William Arthur Ward

*He heals the brokenhearted
and binds their wounds.
Psalm 147:3 NASB*

Tears: the best gift of God to suffering man.
John Keeble

He restores my soul....
Psalm 23:3 NASB

3

Anger and Guilt

The experience of grief is often accompanied by the emotions of anger and guilt. We are understandably angry about our losses, and we may feel guilty about the things that we might have done to prevent them. But beware: Prolonged feelings of anger or guilt have the potential to do great harm.

Anger, left unchecked, tends to invade every aspect of life, eventually transforming itself into bitterness. Irrational guilt, especially over past events that cannot be changed, creates an environment of self-doubt and self-recrimination.

If you are ruled by feelings of anger, guilt, jealousy, fear, or any other negative emotion, understand that these emotions are part of the grieving process. But understand too that hurtful feelings should never become a permanent part of your emotional makeup. God has better things in store for you!

Anger is a natural part of grief,
a constant companion of frustration,
helplessness, and deprivation.
Catherine M. Sanders

Perhaps one of the easiest things to forget
when a husband or wife has died is there
is anger in all loving relationships.
Many mourners find themselves
perplexed by this.
Harriet Sarnoff Schiff

*...The Lord shall give thee rest from thy sorrow,
and from thy fear....
Isaiah 14:3*

No matter how often I read and heard
that anger is a stage of grief, I was sure
that would never happen to me.
Genevieve Davis Ginsburg

Anger at the time of death
is often misdirected at family, friends,
or colleagues.
Helen Fitzgerald

Get wisdom, get understanding; forget it not.
Proverbs 4:5

If your loved one is dead, ask yourself this question: Are you still angry at him?

Wayne Oates

Wise men turn away anger.
Proverbs 29:8 NASB

Be as angry as you
have to be until the day
comes when your
compassion exceeds
your rage.

Ellen Sue Stern

Cease from anger and forsake wrath;
Do not fret; it leads only to evildoing.
Psalm 37:8 NASB

Talk about your feelings of guilt
with someone you trust. Chances are,
what you feel guilty about will have been
experienced by others.
Catherine M. Sanders

When we imagine that if we had acted
differently we might have prevented
the death, we figuratively endow ourselves
with superhuman powers
to change destiny.
Judy Tatelbaum

Happy is he who does not condemn himself....
Romans 14:22 NASB

You may feel guilty when you begin to enjoy life again.

Bob Deits

*I am come that they might have life,
and that they might have it more abundantly.*
John 10:10

Take your burdens of guilt to God and leave them with God.

Wayne Oates

In thee, O Lord, do I put my trust.
Psalm 31:1

4

Grief's Timetable

Once grieving begins, almost everyone wonders: "How long will it last?" There is no universal answer to this question. Different people grieve in different ways. You, therefore, will grieve at your own pace.

Mourning is a process that cannot be hurried; each significant loss is experienced and processed according to its own timetable. But in the darkness of your own particular sorrow, it is imperative to remember that God stands forever ready, always offering His healing hand to you.

When the shock wears off, we begin
to experience the full impact and pain
of facing the finality of our loss.

Judy Tatelbaum

Let us define the stages of grieving
as feelings or emotions or a state of mind,
and know that they come and go
like the tide.

Genevieve Davis Ginsburg

Wait for the Lord; Be strong and
let your heart take courage.
Psalm 27:14 NASB

Each of us deals with grief in a different way and on a different timetable.

Zig Ziglar

To every thing there is a season, and a time to every purpose under the heaven.
Ecclesiastes 3:1

There is wisdom in the traditional one year of mourning, which enables the bereaved to take at least some of the time necessary to experience and complete the grieving process.

Judy Tatelbaum

Many bereaved people call the second year their lonely year.

Bob Deits

Call upon me in the day of trouble: I will deliver thee, and thou shalt glorify me.
Psalm 50:15

Be patient with yourself; grief takes time. You will want to rush the process, but it moves at its own pace.

Catherine M. Sanders

Patience of spirit is better than haughtiness of spirit.
Ecclesiastes 7:8 NASB

There is no grief which time does not lessen and soften.

Cicero

My soul waits for the Lord....
Psalm 130:6 NASB

The greater the loss, the longer
your recovery will be.

Alla Renée Bozarth

The Lord who allows each of us
to grieve differently also knows and
provides precisely what will bring
comfort to our hearts.

Zig Ziglar

*He gives strength to the weary, and to him
who lacks might He increases power.
Isaiah 40:29 NASB*

Time will aid in recovery, but it is time that needs to be used well.... Time spent frantically running from grief will not help.

Helen Fitzgerald

Tribulation brings about perseverance; and perseverance, proven character: and proven character, hope.
Romans 5: 3-4 NASB

Give God thy broken
heart, He will make
it whole.

Edmund Prestwick

*For I will restore health unto thee, and I will heal
thee of thy wounds, saith the Lord.
Jeremiah 30:17*

Successful grief work depends upon
accepting the loss and changes that
will have to take place in our lives.
Catherine M. Sanders

You have a choice in how you respond
to your loss.
James E. Miller

Ye shall know them by their fruits.
Matthew 7:16

Bereavement has a turning point, but it is hard to determine where it is and when we've reached it.

Catherine M. Sanders

Peace I leave with you, my peace I give unto you.
John 14:27

The lowest ebb is the turn of the tide.

Henry Wadsworth Longfellow

God is our refuge and strength,
a very present help in trouble.
Psalm 46:1

Part II
God's Promises

5

God's Healing Hand

Grief is a universal fact of life: No man or woman, no matter how righteous, is exempt. Christians, however, face their grief with the ultimate armor: God's promises. The verses and quotations that follow remind us that God will help heal us if we let Him into our hearts. And the time to let Him in is now.

Our healing from grief
to a very great extent
lies in our daily
communication
with the Lord.

Zig Ziglar

*If any of you lacks wisdom, let him ask
of God ... and it shall be given.*
James 1:5

I would rather walk with God in the dark than go alone in the light.

Mary Gardiner Brainard

God is light, and in Him is no darkness at all.
I John 1:5 NASB

Relying on God has
to begin over again
every day as if nothing
had yet been done.

C. S. Lewis

I will help thee, saith the Lord.
Isaiah 41:14

The more we depend on God, the more dependable we find he is.

Cliff Richards

*Cast thy burden upon the Lord
and He shall sustain thee.*
Psalm 55:22

God provides for those who have trust.
George Herbert

Begin to weave and God will give
the thread.

German Proverb

With God nothing shall be impossible.
Luke 1:37

Call on God but row away
from the rocks.
Ralph Waldo Emerson

When we do our best, we never know
what miracles await.
Helen Keller

Is any thing too hard for the Lord?
Genesis 18:14

Grief puts us into a position to trust
God alone for our healing and restoration.
Zig Ziglar

God heals us through the love and
support of others.
James W. Moore

Thou shalt love thy neighbor as thyself.
Matthew 19:19

Telling your story will be the most
important thing you will do as a mourner,
because in the very act of telling it,
you are putting your life back together.
Glen W. Davidson

Share your thoughts and emotions
with people who care and understand
your grief.
Kathlyn S. Baldwin

*Bear ye one another's burdens and
so fulfill the law of Christ.
Galatians 6:2*

In our periods of deepest grief, we can trust God to prepare someone to come our way to speak a word of love or encouragement.

Zig Ziglar

He healeth the broken in heart,
and bindeth up their wounds.
Psalm 147:3

The only feelings
that do not heal are
the ones you hide.

Henri Nouwen

*Blessed are ye that hunger now: for ye shall be
filled. Blessed are ye that weep now:
for ye shall laugh.*
Luke 6:21

Suppressed grief suffocates.

Ovid

God washes the eyes by tears until they can behold the invisible land where tears shall come no more.

Henry Ward Beecher

I will lift up mine eyes unto the hills, from which cometh my help. My help cometh from the Lord....
Psalm 121:1

Grief drives men into habits of serious reflection; it sharpens the understanding and softens the heart.

John Adams

The soul would have no rainbow had the eyes no tears.

John Vance Cheney

Let not your heart be troubled: ye believe in God, believe also in me.
John 14:1

I shall be richer all my life for this sorrow.

Elisabeth Kübler-Ross

I have learned, in whatsoever state I am,
therewith to be content.
Philippians 4:11

6

The Gift of Faith

Every significant loss carries with it significant pain, but grieving Christians find strength and comfort in their faith. Faith gives assurance in times of doubt; it provides courage during times of fear.

During times of intense grief, wise Christians renew themselves through prayer, through worship, and through a careful study of God's holy word.

No matter what your circumstances, no matter what your grief, remember that no problem is too big for God. Even yours.

I am truly grateful that faith enables me to move past the question of "Why?"

Zig Ziglar

All things are of God.
II Corinthians 5:18

Faith can put
a candle in
the darkest
night.

Margaret Sangster

*Blessed are they that have not seen,
and yet believed.
John 20:29*

The Christian's response
to bereavement
includes both grief
and hope.

Schuyler P. Brown

Faith is the substance of things hoped for,
the evidence of things not seen.
Hebrews 11:1

God is on both sides
of the grave and
nothing can separate us
from God.

James W. Moore

Surely goodness and mercy shall follow me
all the days of my life; and I will dwell
in the house of the Lord for ever.
Psalm 23:6

God allows us to experience the low
points of life in order to teach us lessons
that we could learn in no other way.
C. S. Lewis

Hope is some extraordinary spiritual
grace that God gives us to control
our fears, not to oust them.
Vincent McNabb

Hope thou in God....
Psalm 42:5

God's heavenly plan doesn't always
make earthly sense.

Charles Swindoll

God has led. God will lead.
God is leading!

Unknown

Whoever trusts in the Lord is kept safe.
Proverbs 29:25 NIV

Faith is the antiseptic of the soul.
Walt Whitman

Faith releases life and sets us free.
Harry Emerson Fosdick

Thy faith hath made thee whole.
Mark 5:34

Live by faith until you have faith.

Peter Boehler

Ask, and it shall be given you; seek and ye shall find; knock and it shall be opened unto you.
Matthew 7:7

God's promises are anchors for your soul.

Charles Stanley

The Lord is my shepherd; I shall not want.
Psalm 23:1

Grief brings us to the point of realizing the vastness of our love, and God's love for us.

Zig Ziglar

The truest end of life is to know the life that never ends.

William Penn

For God so loved the world that he gave his only begotten Son, that whosoever believeth in him should not perish, but have everlasting life.
John 3:16

Faith is necessary to victory.

William Hazlitt

Faith that hasn't been tested
can't be trusted.

Adrian Rogers

Faith builds a bridge across the gulf
of death.

Edward Young

The Lord is good to those whose hope is in him,
to the one who seeks him.
Lamentations 3:25 NIV

Faith is the Christian's foundation,
hope is his anchor.

Jeremy Taylor

God doesn't always smooth the path,
but sometimes he puts springs
in the wagon.

Marshall Lucas

He leadeth me in the paths of righteousness
for his name's sake.
Psalm 23:3

God works powerfully, but for the most part gently and gradually.

Unknown

Christianity is the land of beginning again.

W. A. Criswell

The Lord reigns; let the earth rejoice.
Psalm 97:1 NASB

7

Living Again

The Book of Ecclesiastes reminds us that there is a time for everything: a time for grief and a time for healing. Even if you are currently gripped by an overwhelming sense of loss, rest assured: Better days are ahead. The quality of those days depends, in large part, upon the quality of your relationship with your Creator.

If you are grieving, never lose faith in your God or your future. God stands ready to offer His healing hand. So why not take His hand today?

You don't ever completely "get over" profound grief. You incorporate the grief into your life, and you choose to live again.

Bob Powers

Seek the Lord, and ye shall live.
Amos 5:6

Sadness flies away on the wings of time.

Jean de la Fontaine

*Ye shall be sorrowful, but your sorrow
shall be turned into joy.
John 16:20*

Sorrow is a fruit; God does not make
it grow on limbs too weak to bear it.
Victor Hugo

Mourning has its necessities,
but there comes a time when
it should be done with.
John Hinton

A merry heart doeth good like a medicine.
Proverbs 17:22

When God shuts a door, He opens a window.

John Ruskin

Show me thy ways, O Lord; teach me thy paths.
Psalm 25:4

The way out of grief
is through it.

Bob Deits

Salvation is of the Lord.
Jonah 2:9

Each of us can be
a creative survivor.
Judy Tatelbaum

He who stands firm to the end will be saved.
Mark 13:13 NIV

The only way out is ahead, and our
choice is whether we shall cringe from it
or affirm it.

Rollo Ma

Loss can launch the survivor
into a new life.

Judy Tatelbaun

He that hath the Son hath life.
I John 5:12

Perhaps the most important message
is that if you allow yourself to sink,
there will have been a double tragedy.
It is a tragedy you can avert.

Harriet Sarnoff Schiff

Success is finishing what God gave you
to do.

Harold Cook

Teach me thy way, O Lord;
I will walk in thy truth.
Psalm 86:11

Tomorrow will be a new day.
   When God sends the dawn,
      He sends it for all.

Cervante

Be patient toward all that is unresolved
   in your heart and try to love
      the questions themselves.

Rainer Rilk

Let the peace of God rule in your hearts....
Colossians 3:15

Grieving is a process rather than
a series of uphill steps, and gains
are most often realized in retrospect.
Genevieve Davis Ginsburg

You will find your grief producing
growth — a growth that is almost
indiscernible at first.
Carol Stauda

*When I sit in darkness, the Lord shall be
a light unto me.
Micah: 7:8*

In the depletion of your spiritual resource
you have the beginnings of new hope:
All you need is to feel your need of him.
Wayne Oat

No matter how deeply we hurt or how
much pain we suffer in our grief, God has
something good for us in the midst of it.
Zig Zig

*It is good that a man should both hope and quietly
wait for the salvation of the Lord.*
Lamentations 3:26

We come out of grief as deeper persons
because we have been down in
the depths of despair.
Granger Westberg

I walked a mile with sorrow,
and ne'er a word said she;
But, oh, the things I learned from her
When sorrow walked with me.
Robert Browning

The counsel of the Lord standeth forever.
Psalm 33:11

Most of us — to our own amazement — mobilize our inner resources and grow even stronger for having coped.

Genevieve Davis Ginsburg

Be not afraid, neither be thou dismayed: for the Lord thy God is with thee....
Joshua 1:9

Your time of loss can become a time of discovery.

James E. Miller

Give me understanding, and I shall live.
Psalm 119:144

Nothing in this world
is without meaning.

A. W. Tozier

Every grief encounter is an opportunity
to grow.

Charlie Walton

If we endure, we will also reign with Him.
II Timothy: 2:12 NASB

Out of suffering have emerged
the strongest souls; the most massive
characters are seared with scars.
E. H. Chapin

Be hopeful! For tomorrow has never
happened before.
Robert Schuller

*We know that all things work together for good
to them that love God....
Romans 8:28*

God gives quietness at last.

John Greenleaf Whittier

Come unto me, all ye that labor and are heavy laden, and I will give you rest.
Matthew 11:28

Joy is the serious business of heaven.

C. S. Lewis

They that sow in tears shall reap in joy.
Psalm 126:5

Joy is sorrow inside out;
Grief remade again.

Hannah Hurnard

*I sought the Lord, and he heard me, and delivered
me from all my fears.*
Psalm 34:4

Appendix:
Things You Can Do

Marshalling Your Resources

As you work through your grief, you will find it helpful to utilize all the resources that are available to you. God intends that you have a meaningful, abundant life, but He expects you to do your part in claiming His blessings. Thus, it is your responsibility to seek out help when you need it. First and foremost, lean upon the love, help, and support of family, friends, fellow church members, and your pastor. Other resources include:

1. Various local counseling services including, but not limited to, pastoral counselors, psychologists, and community mental health facilities.
2. Group counseling programs which may deal with your specific loss. Talking with others who have experienced a loss similar to yours will be extremely helpful.
3. Your personal physician.
4. The local bookstore or library which contains specific reading material about your grief and about your particular loss.

Holidays and Anniversaries

Holidays, anniversaries, and birthdays are times when memories come flooding back. During these times, you may find yourself dreading the prospect of another "sad day." As these days approach consider the following:

1. Don't try to gloss over or ignore important dates. Instead, prepare yourself for the upcoming events by talking about your feelings with family, trusted friends or counselors.
2. Don't be upset if a particular holiday or anniversary is a sad occasion. And don't for a single minute believe that all future holidays will be lonely. Instead, remind yourself that things will gradually improve with time.
3. If you know a difficult day is looming on the horizon, take the initiative to be with family or friends. Make it your responsibility to contact others, don't wait for them to contact you.
4. Don't feel guilty if you enjoy the holiday or anniversary. Your ability to laugh — even if that laughter is mixed with tears — is a sign that healing has begun. Remember that laughter is one of God's gifts.

Sleep

Periods of grief often result in disturbed sleep or in a total lack of sleep. In such cases, consider the following:

1. Reduce your intake of caffeine or, if needed, eliminate caffeine entirely from your diet. The residual effects of too much coffee or too many soft drinks may be contributing to your sleeplessness.
2. At least one hour before bedtime, begin the process of preparing for sleep by putting yourself into a calmer state. Don't watch television programs that might upset you or "get your juices flowing." Instead, engage in quieter pursuits (such as reading) in order to ready yourself for a good night's sleep. Then, in a more peaceful state, you can fall asleep more easily.
3. If you can't fall asleep quickly, don't lie in bed and worry about the fact that you are not sleeping. Instead, get up, pick up a book, and read until you feel tired. Then go back to bed. Your bed should be a place for sleeping, not a place for worrying.

4. Establish regular sleep patterns by getting up at the same time every day. Even if you don't fall asleep until a very late hour, force yourself out of bed at the same time each morning. This practice will, within a few weeks, help you establish a more normal pattern of sleep.

5. Troubles and worries are always magnified during the nighttime hours. If you are too worried about a particular topic to fall asleep, do not lie in bed and obsess over the problem. Instead, get up, take pencil and paper, and write down your worries along with an action plan to solve them.

6. Engage in sensible physical exercise on a regular basis.

7. If you drink alcohol, drink in moderation. Too much alcohol interrupts normal sleep.

8. If you, or someone close to you, feels that your lack of sleep is posing a hazard to your physical or emotional well-being, consult your physician.

9. Remember the words of Victor Hugo: "Have courage for all the great sorrows of life and patience for the small ones. And when you have finished your daily task, go to sleep. God is awake."

Grief Versus Depression

Grief is a natural response to any significant loss. Grief runs its course and gradually abates over time. Depression, on the other hand, is a physical and emotional condition that is, in almost all cases, treatable by counseling, medication, or both. Left untreated, depression is extremely dangerous to your physical health and to your emotional well-being.

If you have recently experienced a traumatic loss, grief is unavoidable. But if you, or someone close to you, fears that your grief may have evolved into clinical depression, it's time to seek professional help. Consider the following:

1. If you have persistent urges toward self-destructive behavior, or if you feel as though you have lost the will to live, consult a professional counselor or physician immediately.
2. If someone you trust urges you to seek counseling, schedule a session with a professionally trained counselor to evaluate your condition.

3. If you experience persistent and prolonged changes in sleep patterns, or if you experience a significant change in weight (either gain or loss), consult your physician.
4. If you are plagued by consistent, prolonged, severe feelings of hopelessness or apathy, consult a physician or professional counselor.

In summary, depression is a serious but treatable condition. If you suspect that depression may have a grip on you or someone you love, seek professional guidance without delay. As the old saying goes: "Better safe than sorry."

Putting Your Feelings on Paper

You may find it helpful to write down your feelings and memories. Consider the following:

1. You may wish to begin keeping a journal of your thoughts and experiences. As you commit your emotions to paper, you are "working through" your sorrow in a tangible way. Furthermore, you can use your journal as a history of your experiences, thus allowing yourself to gauge the healing that is taking place in your life.

2. You may wish to create a scrapbook of pictures and other reminders of the deceased. The scrapbook is not only a tribute to your loved one, it is also a way of processing your grief.

3. You may wish to compose a letter to the deceased expressing your feelings of love, anger, fear, loss, and hope. This letter may also contain words that you wish you had spoken to the deceased, but didn't.

Finding New Meaning for Living

Perhaps your loss has turned your world upside down. Perhaps everything in your life has been changed forever. Perhaps your relationships and your responsibilities have been permanently altered. If so, you may come face-to-face with the daunting task of finding a new purpose for living.

God has an important plan for your life, and part of His plan may well be related to your grief. Your suffering carries with it great potential: the potential for intense personal growth and the potential to help others. As you begin to reorganize your life, always be watchful for ways to use your suffering for the betterment of others. Lend your experienced hand to help fellow travelers, knowing with assurance that the course of your healing will depend upon how quickly you discover new people to help and new reasons to live.

As you move through and beyond your grief, be mindful of this fact: As a wounded survivor, you will have countless opportunities to serve others. And by serving others, you will bring glory to God and meaning to the suffering you've endured.

Quoted Sources

If You Found This
Book Helpful...

then you will enjoy other books from DELANEY
STREET PRESS and WALNUT GROVE PRESS. For
more information about inspirational books
such as this one, please call 800-256-8584.

About the Author

Criswell Freeman is a Doctor of Clinical Psychology living in Nashville, Tennessee. In addition to this text, Dr. Freeman is also the author of many other books including his bestselling self help book *When Life Throws You a Curveball, Hit It*.

About
DELANEY STREET PRESS

DELANEY STREET PRESS publishes books designed to inspire and entertain readers of all ages. DELANEY STREET books are distributed by WALNUT GROVE PRESS. For more information, call 1-800-256-8584.